AF480673

QUOTES THAT INSPIRE AND EMPOWER

GUIDING WORDS TO LIFT YOUR JOURNEY

DR. MINAKSHI BANSAL

DEDICATION

This book is dedicated to all those who believe in the power of words to inspire change and ignite the human spirit. To the dreamers, the doers, the thinkers, and the believers who face the challenges of everyday life with courage and determination.

To the teachers who ignite curiosity, the mentors who guide with wisdom, the families who support with unwavering love, and the friends who encourage with heartfelt sincerity.

May these pages serve as a beacon of hope and motivation, reminding you that no matter the darkness, the strength to persevere and the light to thrive are always within reach.

▷▷▷

Contents

Contents

Prayer

"Om Bhadram Karnebhih Shrinuyama Devah
Bhadram Pashyemakshabhiryajatrah
Sthirairangais Tushtuvamsastanubhih
Vyashema Devahitam Yadayuh
Svasti Na Indro Vriddhashravah
Svasti Nah Pusha Vishwavedah
Svasti Nastarkshyo Arishtanemih
Svasti No Brihaspatir Dadhatu
Om Shantih Shantih Shantih"

This mantra is a prayer for universal well-being, invoking the blessings of various deities for protection, health, and happiness. It emphasizes the importance of experiencing the auspicious through all senses and living a life aligned with divine purpose. The repetition of "Shantih" at the end signifies a deep desire for peace in the individual, the environment, and the universe at large. This mantra is often recited as a prayer for peace, prosperity, and the physical and spiritual well-being of all beings.

About Theauthor

Dr. Minakshi Bansal, born in the bustling metropolis of Delhi, India, has led a life steeped in artistry, scholarly pursuit, and an unwavering commitment to societal betterment. Following her marriage, she relocated to Ahmedabad, Gujarat, where she has since blossomed into a multifaceted beacon of inspiration for many. Dr. Minakshi is not only recognized as a gifted artist in the realm of Fine Arts but also as an esteemed author, a devoted social worker and a dedicated research scholar in Psychology. Her journey, marked by a profound dedication to elevating those around her, especially the downtrodden and underprivileged children of society, is a testament to her deep-seated belief in the transformative power of engagement and empathy.

From her earliest days, Minakshi was distinguished by an insatiable appetite for reading. Her literary universe was inhabited by characters and narratives that spanned ethical tales, motivational and inspirational stories, and the mythic parables imbued with life lessons. This voracious reading habit was not merely for personal edification but was driven by a desire to distill and disseminate the essence of these narratives to foster the development of students and peers alike. She was particularly captivated by the lives and teachings of historical figures and spiritual leaders such as Adi Shankaracharya, Swami Vivekananda, Dr. APJ Abdul Kalam, Mahamana Pandit Madan Mohan Malviya, Mahatma Gandhi, Sardar Vallabhai Patel, and Vinoba Bhave, among others. Their philosophies and life stories fueled her ambition to embody their ideals of resilience, selflessness, and relentless pursuit of knowledge.

Dr. Minakshi's academic and practical engagement with psychology has been equally noteworthy. As a research scholar, her focus has been on exploring the intricate tapestry of the human psyche, aiming to unlock the potential for psychological well-being and societal harmony. Her scholarly work is complemented by her active involvement in social work, where she employs her academic insights to make tangible differences in the lives of the underprivileged. Her endeavours in social work are characterized by an innovative approach that combines traditional wisdom with contemporary psychological practices to address the multifaceted challenges faced by these communities.

Her artistic talents, another facet of her diverse capabilities, are not merely a personal passion but also serve as a medium through which she communicates and connects with others. Her art, rich in symbolism and emotional depth, reflects her philosophical inquiries and social concerns, offering viewers a glimpse into the breadth of her intellect and the depth of her compassion.

In addition to her contributions to the arts and social sciences, Dr. Minakshi has embraced the healing arts of Pranic Healing, mastering the techniques developed by Master Choa Kok Sui. This practice, which focuses on the manipulation of Prana or life energy to heal the body and aura, has been both a personal journey of discovery and a means through which she extends her healing touch to others. Her proficiency in Pranic Healing is complemented by her advocacy and teaching of various forms of meditation aimed at rejuvenation, personal betterment, and the cultivation of harmony within individuals and communities alike.

Dr. Minakshi's life is a narrative of relentless pursuit, not just of personal achievement but of the upliftment and empowerment of society at large. Her diverse interests and talents—spanning the arts, literature, psychology, and the healing practices—converge on a singular path of service. She embodies the spirit of the luminaries who inspired her, channelling their legacy through her actions and teachings. Through her books, art, and social initiatives, she continues to inspire a new generation to embark on their own journeys of self-discovery, resilience, and altruism.

Her commitment to social betterment, particularly her focus on uplifting underprivileged children, reflects a deep understanding of the transformative potential of education and personal development. By integrating her knowledge of psychology, her artistic sensibilities, and her healing practices, Dr. Bansal has developed a holistic approach to social work that addresses both the immediate needs and the long-term well-being of the communities she serves.

As an author, Dr. Minakshi's writings offer a blend of inspirational insights, practical wisdom, and reflective contemplations drawn from her extensive reading and life experiences. Her books serve as a guide for those seeking to navigate the complexities of life with grace, resilience, and purpose. Through her narratives, she extends an invitation to her readers to explore the depths of their own potential and to contribute meaningfully to the collective well-being of society.

In Dr. Minakshi Bansal, we find a remarkable synthesis of the artist, the scholar, the healer, and the social activist. Her life's work stands as a beacon of hope and a source of inspiration for individuals seeking to make a difference in the world. Her story is a compelling reminder of the power of individual action, rooted in compassion and driven by a profound commitment to the betterment of humanity. Dr. Minakshi's legacy is not just in the tangible outcomes of her efforts but in the enduring spirit of inquiry, empathy, and service that she embodies.

ᏕᏕᏕ

Preface

In the mosaic of human experience, words hold a power unmatched by any other force. They have the ability to inspire, motivate, challenge, and transform. It is with this understanding and a spirit of earnest exploration that I have compiled this collection of hundreds of motivational and inspiring quotes, designed to touch upon the myriad aspects of life—from career and education to relationships, personal motivation, and the echoes of legendary wisdom.

This book, an anthology of carefully selected quotations, is not merely a repository of words. It is a curation of guidance, a compass of sorts, aimed at enlightening paths and enriching minds. Each quote has been chosen not only for its surface beauty but for the deeper resonance it may find within the heart of the reader. Whether you are a seeker of personal inspiration, a student thirsty for educational wisdom, a professional in pursuit of excellence, or someone navigating the complex web of relationships, there is something in this collection for you.

The idea of assembling such a compilation arose from a series of personal reflections and professional interactions that highlighted a common thread—everyone is in search of a spark. Sometimes, all it takes to ignite one's journey is a simple set of the right words at the right moment. This book aims to be a reservoir of these sparks, offering words of encouragement and insight that have stood the test of time, spoken by those who have walked diverse paths and left trails of success.

Career: In the realm of career development, where ambition meets reality, the words you will find here serve as both anchor and sail. They are drawn from industry leaders, pioneers of change, and those who have carved niches of success through relentless endeavor. These quotes aim to guide the professional spirit, offering wisdom on perseverance, innovation, and the art of leadership.

Education: For the realm of education, which shapes minds and forms the foundation of futures, the quotes selected resonate with the power of knowledge and the importance of continual learning and curiosity. They come from educators, philosophers, and life-long learners who remind us that education is not confined within the walls of institutions but is a vast, expansive endeavor that spans a lifetime.

Relationships: In addressing relationships, this collection touches on the core of human interaction—trust, love, respect, and mutual growth. The quotes offer reflections from psychologists, literary figures, and everyday people who have expressed profound insights into forming and sustaining meaningful connections with others.

Motivation and Inspiration: At the heart of this book lie the sections on motivation and inspiration. These quotes are meant to serve as catalysts for action and thought, drawn from motivational speakers, historical figures, and modern-day philosophers whose lives and works have been dedicated to uplifting others.

Legendary Quotes: Finally, the legendary quotes included herein offer timeless wisdom that transcends the ages. These are words that have been spoken in various contexts but continue to inspire and provoke thought across generations and geographical boundaries.

Creating this book was a journey in itself—a journey through ideas, eras, and the human experience. Each quote was selected after sifting through thousands, ensuring that what you read is not just information, but transformation. It is my hope that this book will not only be read but will also be lived; that these quotes will not just be passed by but will prompt action, encourage reflection, and spark joy.

As you turn the pages, may you find the words that resonate with your current needs and future aspirations. May these quotes comfort you, challenge you, and above all, inspire you to live a life of purpose and passion. This book is a tribute to the power of words and an invitation to you, the reader, to continue the dialogue that each quote begins.

With this preface, I invite you on a journey of exploration and inspiration. Let each page you turn enrich your understanding and expand your horizons, and may the paths you choose be brighter for the wisdom shared within these pages. Thank you for picking up this collection, and may it serve as a valuable companion on your journey through the intricacies and wonders of life.

Dr. Minakshi Bansal
Social Activist
Ahmedabad, Gujarat, Bharat

ONE

THE POWER OF POSSIBILITY: NELSON MANDELA & HELEN KELLER

Nelson Mandela and Helen Keller are towering figures whose lives and words offer profound lessons in hope and resilience. Mandela, enduring 27 years of imprisonment in apartheid South Africa, emerged not with bitterness but with messages of forgiveness and understanding. He famously said, "The greatest glory in living lies not in never falling, but in rising every time we fall." This sentiment captures his indomitable spirit and has inspired countless individuals to maintain hope and strength in the face of severe adversity.

Similarly, Helen Keller, who became blind and deaf due to an early childhood illness, demonstrated that physical limitations do not necessarily limit one's capacity for achievement and impact. Her ability to learn and communicate effectively, despite her disabilities, challenged societal perceptions about the disabled.

Her quote, "Optimism is the faith that leads to achievement. Nothing can be done without hope and confidence," reflects her approach to life, emphasizing that inner strength and a positive outlook are crucial for overcoming challenges.

Mahatma Gandhi and Martin Luther King Jr. are also figures synonymous with transformative change and the power of nonviolent resistance. Gandhi's philosophy of nonviolent protest not only led India to independence but also inspired movements for civil rights and freedom across the world. His statement, "You must be the change you wish to see in the world," encourages personal responsibility in the quest for social justice.

King, similarly, fought for civil rights in the United States with a deep commitment to nonviolence, believing that "Darkness cannot drive out darkness; only light can do that. Hate cannot drive out hate; only love can do that." His leadership during the Montgomery Bus Boycott and the subsequent movements underscored the power of collective action guided by a commitment to equity and justice.

In the realm of innovation, Steve Jobs and Marie Curie stand out. Jobs, co-founder of Apple Inc., was instrumental in revolutionizing the technology industry, emphasizing the importance of design and user experience. His encouragement to "Stay hungry, stay foolish," has motivated many to pursue their visions with relentless curiosity.

Marie Curie, the pioneering scientist who discovered radium and polonium, showed unmatched dedication to science, becoming the first woman to win a Nobel Prize. Her journey underscored the idea that perseverance is critical, a concept she embraced when she noted, "Be less curious about people and more curious about ideas."

Artistically, Frida Kahlo and Leonardo da Vinci each explored the depths of human experience and emotion. Kahlo, through her self-portraits and personal plights with health issues, explored themes of identity, postcolonialism, gender, class, and race in Mexican society. One of her powerful quotes, "I paint my own reality," speaks to the authenticity and introspection that defines her work.

Leonardo da Vinci, a polymath of the Renaissance era, left a legacy that encompasses art, science, and invention, reflecting his belief in the interconnectedness of art and nature, famously stating, "Learn how to see. Realize that everything connects to everything else."

The teachings on compassion and mindfulness by Thich Nhat Hanh and the Dalai Lama offer profound insights into the art of living peacefully and purposefully. Thich Nhat Hanh, a Zen master and peace activist, teaches the importance of present moment awareness and loving kindness with sayings such as, "Peace is every step." The Dalai Lama, spiritual leader of the Tibetan people, similarly focuses on the importance of happiness and compassion, famously noting, "My religion is very simple. My religion is kindness."

Muhammad Ali and Serena Williams, both phenomenal athletes, also embody the spirit of resilience and self-belief. Ali's poetic trash-talking and profound sayings, like "I am the greatest, I said that even before I knew I was," demonstrate his unwavering confidence and mental strength.

Serena Williams, one of the most dominant tennis players of all time, has continuously spoken about the power of self-belief and determination in achieving success, famously asserting, "The success of every woman should be the inspiration to another. We should raise each other up."

These legendary figures, through their lives and words, provide timeless wisdom. Their quotes not only inspire but also teach us about the enduring power of human spirit, the importance of maintaining hope in adversity, and the transformative power of believing in oneself. These messages are crucial, not just for personal success, but in inspiring others to act with courage, compassion, and conviction in their journeys.

ᗡᗡᗡ

"Nelson Mandela taught us that our deepest fears can be conquered by embracing love and forgiveness, even against those who have wronged us. His life reminds us that true strength lies in the ability to unify, not divide. Let his legacy inspire us to transform our world with reconciliation and peace."

♡♡♡

TWO

VISIONARIES OF CHANGE: MAHATMA GANDHI & MARTIN LUTHER KING JR.

Mahatma Gandhi and Martin Luther King Jr. are seminal figures in the history of the 20th century, not only for their indelible impacts on their respective countries but also for their profound influence on the global discourse surrounding civil rights, nonviolence, and social change. Their legacies, enriched by their eloquent speeches and writings, continue to inspire movements for justice and peace worldwide.

Mahatma Gandhi's philosophy of nonviolent resistance, or Satyagraha, was revolutionary in its assertion that oppressive systems could be opposed without violence. This radical idea emerged from his deep commitment to ahimsa, or non-harm, rooted in ancient Indian traditions. Gandhi's approach was not merely a political strategy but a comprehensive philosophy encompassing all aspects of life.

His famous maxim, "Be the change you wish to see in the world," encapsulates his belief that personal and societal transformation are interconnected, and that true change begins with oneself. Through this lens, Gandhi led India to independence from British rule, all the while emphasizing the spiritual and moral development of the individual.

Parallel to Gandhi's leadership on the Asian continent, Martin Luther King Jr. emerged as a formidable leader of the Civil Rights Movement in the United States. Inspired by Gandhi's success in India, King adapted the principles of nonviolent protest to the struggle against racial segregation and discrimination in the U.S. His leadership of the Montgomery Bus Boycott, his pivotal role in the March on Washington, and his impactful protests in Birmingham are standout moments where nonviolence was tested but ultimately prevailed, proving its efficacy and moral power.

King eloquently captured the essence of this philosophy in his assertion that, "Nonviolence is a powerful and just weapon. Indeed, it is a weapon unique in history, which cuts without wounding and ennobles the man who wields it."

Both leaders also recognized the importance of suffering in the struggle for justice. Gandhi's numerous fasts and periods of imprisonment were integral to his method of showing the injustices of colonial rule, aiming to awaken the conscience of the oppressor and the oppressed alike. Similarly, King's willingness to endure jail time, as expressed in his famous "Letter from Birmingham Jail," highlighted the pervasive injustices facing African Americans and the need for urgent action. He famously stated, "Injustice anywhere is a threat to justice everywhere."

Their teachings and actions have left a lasting imprint on the fabric of global social movements. The concept of peaceful protest has become a cornerstone of democratic societies, influencing diverse struggles from anti-apartheid movements in South Africa to pro-democracy protests in various parts of the world. The enduring relevance of their words and philosophies is evident as new generations of activists cite Gandhi's and King's teachings in their efforts to advocate for environmental justice, economic equality, and human rights.

Furthermore, both figures underscored the power of love and forgiveness in their campaigns. Gandhi's idea that an opponent must be converted rather than defeated and King's belief in the redemptive power of love are profound teachings that challenge conventional notions of political struggle. They taught that enduring peace cannot be achieved through hatred or revenge but through understanding and reconciliation.

Gandhi's impact on global peace movements and King's influence on civil rights have also been recognized in their call for economic and social rights. Gandhi's advocacy for the poor and his critique of industrial capitalism in favor of a more sustainable village-centered economy resonate today in debates about sustainable development and economic justice.

King's later years were increasingly focused on combating economic inequality, a mission encapsulated in his planning of the Poor People's Campaign.

The philosophies and methods of Mahatma Gandhi and Martin Luther King Jr. represent a profound moral and ethical framework for dealing with the world's perennial problems. Their lives remind us that real change requires patience, sacrifice, and an unshakeable belief in the principles of justice and equality.

As the world continues to face challenges of inequality, discrimination, and environmental crisis, the teachings of these two visionaries of change remain as relevant and inspiring as ever. Their legacy is not confined to the past; it is a living, breathing inspiration for peace and justice movements around the globe.

ppp

"Helen Keller showed the world that physical limitations could never constrain the spirit of a determined soul. Through darkness and silence, she illuminated the power of knowledge and communication. Her courage teaches us that with perseverance and belief, every barrier can be overcome."

THREE

PIONEERS OF INNOVATION: STEVE JOBS & MARIE CURIE

Steve Jobs and Marie Curie, though separated by time and disciplines, share pivotal roles as pioneers of innovation in their respective fields. Their groundbreaking contributions—Jobs in technology and Curie in science—have not only revolutionized their industries but have also provided deep insights that continue to influence and inspire generations to innovate and persevere against all odds.

Marie Curie's work laid the foundations of modern physics and changed the world of medicine. Her research was instrumental in the development of X-ray machines, and she was the first person to win Nobel Prizes in two different scientific disciplines. Curie's life was marked by her relentless pursuit of knowledge, despite numerous obstacles. She once noted, "One never notices what has been done; one can only see what remains to be done." This reflection captures her constant drive to push beyond established boundaries. Her perseverance in the face of adversity, including battling sexism in the scientific community and dealing with the physical toll of her research, speaks volumes about her dedication and resilience.

Similarly, Steve Jobs's impact on technology and consumer electronics is unparalleled. As a co-founder of Apple Inc., he was instrumental in redefining the tech landscape with the introduction of products such as the iPod, iPhone, and iPad, which blended technology with artistry. Jobs was known for his perfectionist attitude and a keen eye for design, insisting that technology should be both functional and intuitive. His vision for Apple was deeply rooted in the belief that design and usability are paramount, famously stating, "Design is not just what it looks like and feels like. Design is how it works." Jobs's approach to innovation was holistic, seeing it as the intersection of technology and liberal arts.

Both Curie and Jobs faced significant challenges on their paths to success. Curie's work with radioactive materials, while pioneering, was perilous. She and her husband worked under poor laboratory conditions, not fully aware of the dangers posed by radiation. Despite suffering from health issues likely caused by radiation exposure, Curie never ceased her work, driven by the belief that scientific discovery was a noble pursuit that could significantly benefit humanity. This commitment is reflected in her dedication to her research and her decision to not patent her processes, which enabled other scientists to further their own research freely.

On the other hand, Steve Jobs's journey with Apple was not without its setbacks. He was famously ousted from the company in 1985, only to return more than a decade later and lead Apple to become one of the most valuable companies in the world. His resilience during his years away from Apple, including founding NeXT and revitalizing Pixar Animation Studios, showcased his ability to innovate across different fields. Jobs's philosophy was that true innovation often requires facing failures and setbacks. His return to Apple and subsequent successes with innovative products underscored his belief in persistence, vision, and the importance of following one's intuition. He emphasized that "You have to trust in something—your gut, destiny, life, karma, whatever," a mantra that guided his career decisions.

The legacies of Marie Curie and Steve Jobs are not just in their individual achievements but also in their approach to work and problem-solving. They both demonstrated that innovation is not simply about having a good idea but also about the perseverance to see it through despite challenges. They showed that revolutionary breakthroughs often require going against the consensus and forging one's path.

Furthermore, both Curie and Jobs shared a profound commitment to their visions, which were rooted in bettering human lives through science and technology. Curie's work has had a lasting impact on medical treatments, and Jobs's innovations have transformed the way people interact with technology. Their lives remind us that at the heart of innovation lies a deep-seated desire to challenge the status quo and push the boundaries of what is possible.

Their stories are a testament to the fact that the journey of innovation is fraught with challenges, but it is these very challenges that often lead to the greatest breakthroughs. Curie and Jobs not only changed the landscape of their respective fields but also left behind a legacy of inspiration for future generations to continue pushing the envelope, to keep innovating, and to persevere in the face of adversity. Their lives and work exemplify the essence of innovation and continue to motivate those looking to make a significant impact in any field.

ppp

"Mahatma Gandhi's philosophy of non-violence and truth challenged and changed an empire. He demonstrated that the power of peaceful protest is stronger than any force of oppression. Let his wisdom guide us to pursue justice and equality through patience and resilience."

▷▷▷

FOUR

RTISTS OF LIFE: FRIDA KAHLO & LEONARDO DA VINCI

Frida Kahlo and Leonardo da Vinci, each in their own era and with their distinct styles, dramatically reshaped the understanding of art's role in expressing the human condition. Their works, deeply infused with personal and universal themes, continue to captivate and provoke audiences, offering rich insights into the intricacies of human life and the boundless possibilities of creativity.

Frida Kahlo, a Mexican painter known for her striking self-portraits, used her canvas as a battlefield to explore complex personal and societal issues. Living through physical pain and emotional turmoil, Kahlo's art reflects her life's struggles, including her troubled marriage, her numerous health issues, and her deep concerns with identity, postcolonialism, and the human body. Her ability to convey raw emotional depth and her bold visual style make her work profoundly compelling. She once said, "I never paint dreams or nightmares. I paint my own reality." This statement encapsulates her approach to art as a means of personal truth-telling and survival, making her work intensely personal yet universally relatable. Each stroke and color choice reveals her inner world and invites viewers to confront the complexities of their own identities and experiences.

Leonardo da Vinci, a polymath of the Italian Renaissance, remains a towering figure in the history of art due to his meticulous studies of the human body, nature, and mechanics, which informed his artistic work. His curiosity and boundless pursuit of knowledge led him to fill thousands of pages of notebooks with observations, sketches, and theories. Works like the "Mona Lisa" and "The Last Supper" not only showcase his mastery of technique but also his profound understanding of human psychology and emotion. Da Vinci believed that art was connected deeply to all aspects of life, famously stating, "Art is the queen of all sciences communicating knowledge to all the generations of the world." This reflects his belief in the power of art to encapsulate and communicate human experience and knowledge.

Both artists shared a common understanding of art as a reflection of life. Kahlo's use of vivid colors and symbolic imagery in her self-portraits communicates her pain, her passions, and her cultural heritage, inviting onlookers into her lived experience. She depicted her realities without reservation, challenging societal norms about femininity, beauty, and suffering. Her portraits are a dialogue with the viewer, a bold statement of existence and resistance.

Da Vinci's approach to art was analytical yet deeply expressive. His scientific studies, especially in anatomy, enabled him to bring lifelike accuracy and emotion to his figures. His detailed dissections of the human body enhanced his ability to portray human anatomy with remarkable precision, which was revolutionary at the time. His drawings and paintings do not merely replicate physical appearances; they capture the subtleties of human expression and emotion, making the figures seem alive, filled with potential for movement and thought.

Moreover, both Kahlo and Da Vinci extended their artistic pursuits beyond traditional boundaries. Kahlo's exploration of gender, politics, and personal identity in a conservative society was pioneering. Her art became a tool for exploring and asserting identity in ways that were ahead of her time. She is often seen as an icon of feminism and resilience, using her personal plight and cultural background to challenge and redefine contemporary notions of beauty and strength.

In contrast, da Vinci's work transcended the realms of art, science, and invention. His visionary projects, ranging from the designs of flying machines to hydraulic systems, show that his artistic vision was not confined to canvas but was an expansive force that sought to understand and reimagine the world. His relentless curiosity and innovative spirit drove him to investigate the laws of science and nature, which in turn enriched his artistic output.

The legacy of Frida Kahlo and Leonardo da Vinci is profound. They inspire not only artists but anyone who seeks to understand the depths of human experience and the power of creativity as a means of expression and exploration. Their lives and works demonstrate that art is not just a form of aesthetic creation but a vital means of engaging with and interpreting the world. Through their innovative spirits and deep introspections, they have permanently imprinted on art history a vibrant narrative of life's fragility, beauty, complexity, and the endless pursuit of understanding.

ԵԵԵ

"Martin Luther King Jr.'s dream reshaped a nation and redefined generations. His words, a blend of eloquence and prophetic insight, continue to challenge us to judge not by the color of our skin, but by the content of our character. May his vision of equality and justice inspire us to keep moving toward a world where freedom rings for everyone."

▷▷▷

FIVE

WARRIORS OF MINDFULNESS: THICH NHAT HANH & DALAI LAMA

Thich Nhat Hanh and the Dalai Lama stand as beacons of wisdom and peace in a tumultuous world, teaching millions the principles of mindfulness, compassion, and spiritual growth. Through their teachings, both have imparted profound insights on how to live a life enriched with meaningful connections and a peaceful mind, influencing not only individual lives but also global peace initiatives.

Thich Nhat Hanh, a Vietnamese Zen master and peace activist, has been a pioneer in bringing mindfulness to the West. His approach to mindfulness is deeply practical, advocating for "mindfulness in every action." From the simple act of breathing to the complex interactions of daily life, he teaches that mindfulness is the key to deeper understanding and peace. His famous phrase, "The present moment is filled with joy and happiness. If you are attentive, you will see it," encapsulates his philosophy that happiness is accessible in the simplicity of the present moment, not somewhere distant in the future.

Similarly, the Dalai Lama, the spiritual leader of the Tibetan people, has emphasized the importance of compassion as essential to human survival. His teachings often focus on the interconnectedness of all beings and the necessity of caring for others' well-being as the foundation of a healthy society and personal happiness. He frequently states, "If you want others to be happy, practice compassion. If you want to be happy, practice compassion," highlighting the dual benefit of compassion to both giver and receiver.

Both leaders have drawn from their rich traditions—Buddhist teachings that date back thousands of years—to address modern problems. Thich Nhat Hanh introduced the concept of "Engaged Buddhism," which applies Buddhist insights to social, political, environmental, and economic suffering. He has shown that mindfulness is not just a personal practice but one that can profoundly affect the world, emphasizing that understanding and mindful communication can resolve conflicts. Through his teachings and numerous books, he has offered techniques that help individuals deal with anger, anxiety, and misunderstanding, promoting a culture of peace.

The Dalai Lama, exiled from Tibet since 1959, has become a global symbol of peace and resilience. His teachings often explore the concept of "universal responsibility," the idea that each person has a role in creating a better world. His discussions on the science of happiness have bridged Eastern and Western thought, showing how ancient Buddhist concepts of mindfulness and compassion align with contemporary scientific studies on happiness and well-being. His dialogue with scientists has helped promote a greater understanding of the mind and its role in emotional and spiritual health.

The influence of Thich Nhat Hanh and the Dalai Lama extends beyond their spiritual teachings, impacting global humanitarian and peace efforts. Thich Nhat Hanh's life, for instance, includes tireless activism during the Vietnam War, advocating for peace and reconciliation between the conflicting sides. His nomination by Martin Luther King Jr. for the Nobel Peace Prize in 1967 acknowledges his efforts to integrate mindfulness and social action.

The Dalai Lama's commitment to non-violence and his stance on Tibetan autonomy have earned him the Nobel Peace Prize in 1989. His enduring message that "Peace does not mean an absence of conflicts; differences will always be there. Peace means solving these differences through peaceful means; through dialogue, education, knowledge; and through humane ways," serves as a guiding light for conflict resolution and diplomacy.

Through their teachings on mindfulness and compassion, both Thich Nhat Hanh and the Dalai Lama offer more than just methods for personal serenity; they provide a blueprint for constructing a compassionate society. They teach that true spiritual growth involves recognizing and responding to the suffering of others, crafting a life that extends beyond personal fulfillment to encompass care and concern for all beings.

Their lessons in mindfulness and compassion demonstrate that personal and spiritual growth are deeply interconnected with how individuals engage with the world. By fostering empathy, promoting peace, and encouraging a mindful presence in all activities, they offer a path not only to personal contentment but to greater societal harmony. Their lives and teachings remind us that each person's inner transformation can contribute to a more peaceful and compassionate world, echoing the profound truth that the nature of human existence is deeply interconnected.

ॐॐॐ

"Steve Jobs reminded us that innovation doesn't just change the way we do things—it changes the way we see the world. He believed that people with passion can change the world for the better. May his pursuit of excellence inspire us to always seek the innovative and the incredible."

▷▷▷

SIX

CHAMPIONS OF WILLPOWER: MUHAMMAD ALI & SERENA WILLIAMS

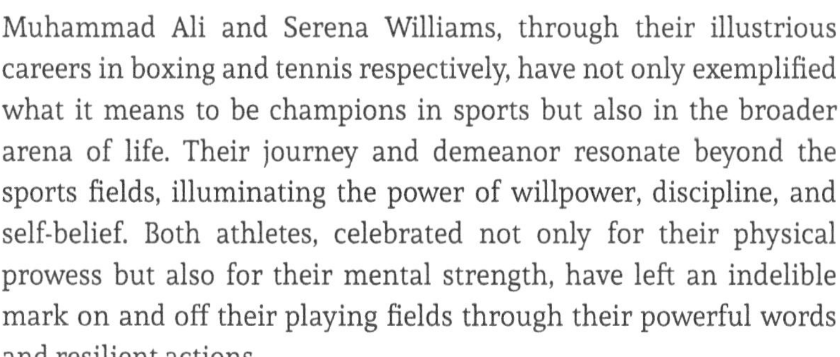

Muhammad Ali and Serena Williams, through their illustrious careers in boxing and tennis respectively, have not only exemplified what it means to be champions in sports but also in the broader arena of life. Their journey and demeanor resonate beyond the sports fields, illuminating the power of willpower, discipline, and self-belief. Both athletes, celebrated not only for their physical prowess but also for their mental strength, have left an indelible mark on and off their playing fields through their powerful words and resilient actions.

Muhammad Ali, often celebrated as "The Greatest," was known for his flamboyant and unapologetic personality, both inside and outside the boxing ring. His psychological warfare and poetic trash-talking preceding fights were as strategic as they were entertaining, serving to intimidate opponents while bolstering his own self-belief. Ali's famous proclamation, "I am the greatest, I said that even before I knew I was," is not merely a boast but a manifestation of the profound self-confidence that he believed was essential to his success. This declaration became a self-fulfilling prophecy, as his unyielding belief in his own greatness propelled him to become one of the most legendary figures in the world of sports.

Ali's resilience was not limited to his verbal affirmations; it was demonstrated profoundly when he faced seemingly insurmountable odds. One of his most iconic fights, the 1974 "Rumble in the Jungle" against the formidable George Foreman, showcased Ali's strategic genius and mental toughness. Ali, considered an underdog, withstood a barrage of powerful blows using what he called the "rope-a-dope" strategy, absorbing punishment while conserving energy to make a comeback later in the fight. His victory stunned the world and exemplified his strategic acumen and sheer willpower. Beyond the ring, Ali's activism, particularly his stand against the Vietnam War and his vocal support for civil rights, underscored his courage and commitment to his principles, further solidifying his status as a champion of the people.

Similarly, Serena Williams has dominated the world of tennis with her extraordinary talent and unrelenting determination. Williams, who emerged from humble beginnings, has shattered countless barriers in a sport historically dominated by athletes who did not look like her. Her journey to becoming one of the greatest tennis players of all time is a testament to her incredible work ethic and belief in her own abilities. Williams once said, "The success of every woman should be the inspiration to another. We should raise each other up," reflecting her understanding of her role not just as a competitor but as a mentor and role model.

Williams's career has been marked by numerous comebacks, from life-threatening health issues to the challenges of motherhood, each time returning to the top of her game. Her 2017 Australian Open victory while pregnant is a striking example of her indomitable spirit and physical resilience. Her ability to compete at the highest levels, against much younger opponents, while balancing family life and business ventures, showcases her multifaceted strength and commitment to excellence.

Both Ali and Williams have used their platforms to inspire others, not just through their achievements but through their words and actions off the playing field. They have advocated for social issues and encouraged countless individuals to believe in themselves, fight against adversity, and pursue their dreams with unwavering determination. Their quotes and speeches often serve as motivational mantras for those looking to cultivate discipline and self-belief.

The legacy of Muhammad Ali and Serena Williams extends far beyond their sports. They exemplify how discipline, confidence, and the power of self-belief are not merely ingredients for success in sports but are universally applicable principles that can guide personal and professional achievements. They remind us that the mind is just as important as the body in overcoming obstacles and achieving greatness. Through their lives and words, they continue to motivate individuals around the world to strive for their best, persist through difficulties, and believe in their own potential, regardless of the challenges they face. Their stories are not just about sports; they are about the enduring human spirit's capacity to triumph over adversity.

ppp

"Marie Curie's dedication to science illuminated the mysteries of nature and the power of persistence. Her journey reminds us that curiosity must often be coupled with courage. Let her legacy motivate us to never stop questioning and exploring the world around us."

❦❦❦

SEVEN

STRATEGISTS OF SUCCESS: SUN TZU & WARREN BUFFETT

Sun Tzu, an ancient Chinese military strategist, and Warren Buffett, an American business magnate and investor, represent two vastly different eras and fields, yet both are quintessential examples of strategic mastery. Their teachings and practices provide invaluable lessons in planning and decision-making that transcend their immediate domains of military conflict and investment.

Sun Tzu, who lived during the Eastern Zhou period of ancient China, is best known for his work "The Art of War," a treatise on military strategy and tactics. This work has endured not only as a guide for military leaders but also as a source of wisdom for individuals in various fields, including business and sports, who seek to understand the dynamics of competition and conflict resolution. One of his most quoted lines, "All warfare is based on deception," highlights the importance of strategy over brute force, suggesting that winning involves anticipating and outthinking an opponent rather than overpowering them.

Sun Tzu's approach to military engagements was highly methodical and psychological. He emphasized the importance of knowing oneself as well as one's enemy, a philosophy encapsulated in his assertion, "If you know the enemy and know yourself, you need not fear the result of a hundred battles." This idea of preparedness extends beyond the battlefield; it underscores the universal need for self-awareness and understanding of one's environment in any strategic endeavor. Sun Tzu also promoted the concept of strategic flexibility—adapting to changing conditions and seizing opportunities as they arise. His strategies were not about rigid plans but about dynamic responses to fluid situations.

Warren Buffett, often called the "Oracle of Omaha," has become a symbol of investment success with a philosophy that emphasizes long-term investment strategies, value investing, and financial prudence. Buffett's approach to investing is grounded in the principles taught by Benjamin Graham—known as the father of value investing—which focus on fundamental analysis to evaluate the intrinsic value of a company, thereby identifying undervalued stocks. Buffett's famous adage, "Be fearful when others are greedy, and greedy when others are fearful," reflects his contrarian approach to investing, encapsulating his knack for going against market trends to make investment decisions based on underlying business value and not on speculative pressures.

Buffett's strategic acumen extends beyond choosing which stocks to buy; it also involves deciding when to buy and when to sell, maintaining a disciplined approach to capital allocation, and understanding the market cycles. His success is largely attributed to his extraordinary patience and his ability to think independently. He has often highlighted the importance of temperament in investing, suggesting that being able to control one's emotions and think long-term are crucial components of financial success.

Both Sun Tzu and Buffett have demonstrated that at the core of effective strategy lies the capacity for critical thinking and decision-making under uncertainty. Sun Tzu's military strategies involve an acute analysis of geopolitical landscapes, enemy capabilities, logistical considerations, and moral factors. Similarly, Buffett's investment decisions are based on a thorough analysis of financial statements, understanding of industry trends, and evaluation of company leadership and governance.

Moreover, both figures embody the principle of ethical leadership. Sun Tzu argued for the humane treatment of captured soldiers and the importance of building moral harmony within one's ranks, reflecting his belief in ethical considerations in leadership. Likewise, Buffett is known for his ethical business practices, his philanthropic efforts, and his advocacy for responsible wealth accumulation and redistribution.

The strategic teachings of Sun Tzu and Warren Buffett, though separated by millennia and context, converge on the essential elements of successful strategy—knowledge, preparation, patience, flexibility, and ethical consideration. These principles serve as fundamental guides not only for military leaders and investors but for anyone who must make decisions in the face of competition and conflict. Their lessons on planning and decision-making resonate across ages, offering timeless wisdom for navigating the complexities of modern life and achieving sustained success.

"Frida Kahlo turned her pain into a vibrant testament to life, proving that art could be both personal and universally impactful. Her canvases, rich with color and emotion, challenge us to confront our own realities. May her strength inspire us to create beauty from our battles."

ᗞᗞᗞ

EIGHT

MASTERS OF LITERATURE: MAYA ANGELOU & WILLIAM SHAKESPEARE

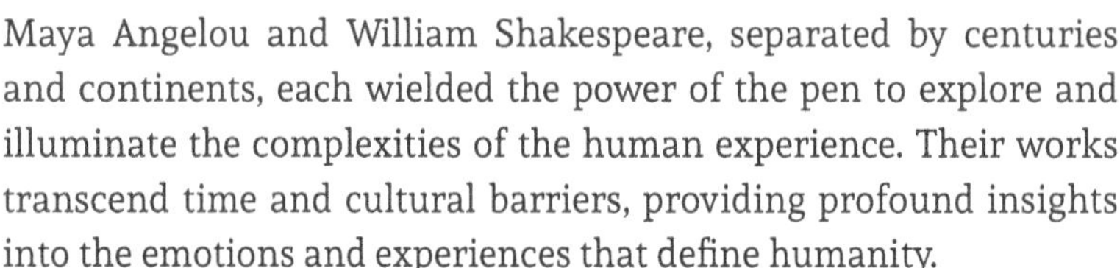

Maya Angelou and William Shakespeare, separated by centuries and continents, each wielded the power of the pen to explore and illuminate the complexities of the human experience. Their works transcend time and cultural barriers, providing profound insights into the emotions and experiences that define humanity.

William Shakespeare, often referred to as the Bard of Avon, is hailed as one of the greatest playwrights in the English language. His vast body of work, including tragedies, comedies, and histories, delves deeply into the human psyche, exploring themes of love, power, jealousy, betrayal, and ambition. Shakespeare's ability to articulate the depth of human emotion and experience is perhaps unmatched. His characters are timeless, their struggles and conflicts resonantly universal. In "Hamlet," he explores the depths of grief and despair, encapsulated in the prince's soliloquy, "To be, or not to be," which ponders the value of life in the face of suffering. Through Macbeth's ambition and Lady Macbeth's guilt, Shakespeare examines the corrupting power of unchecked ambition and the profound effects of remorse.

Shakespeare's genius lies not only in his storytelling but in his mastery of the English language, which remains influential. He had a unique ability to coin new phrases and words, many of which have become integral parts of the language. His works challenge the reader's understanding of human nature and social dynamics, making them a staple in discussions of ethical and philosophical issues. His poetic expressions, such as "All the world's a stage, And all the men and women merely players," from "As You Like It," reflect his perception of life as transient and roles as temporary, an insight that invites reflection on the nature of existence and our behaviors within it.

Maya Angelou, an American poet, memoirist, and civil rights activist, brought a powerful and poignant voice to the discussion of race, identity, and the human condition. Her series of seven autobiographies, beginning with "I Know Why the Caged Bird Sings," narrates her struggles with racism, trauma, and identity, weaving a rich tapestry of emotional depth that resonates with a wide audience. Angelou's ability to convey complex emotions and experiences in simple yet profound language makes her works both accessible and deeply moving.

Her poetry often serves as a clarion call for justice and equality, sung with a rhythm that draws heavily on her African American heritage and oral traditions. In her inaugural poem, "On the Pulse of Morning," presented at President Bill Clinton's inauguration, Angelou speaks of hope and change, urging the nation to embrace unity and collective progress. Her line, "The horizon leans forward, offering you space to place new steps of change," encapsulates her optimistic vision of the future and the potential for personal and societal growth.

Both Angelou and Shakespeare explored themes of resilience in the face of adversity. Angelou's writings often reflect her personal experiences with discrimination and violence, yet they also emphasize survival and empowerment. Her declaration, "But still, like air, I'll rise," from her poem "Still I Rise," serves as a powerful testament to the indomitable human spirit. Similarly, Shakespeare's characters frequently face dire situations, yet his plays often provide catharsis and insights into the strength of character, such as through the resilience of Portia in "The Merchant of Venice" or Viola in "Twelfth Night."

The works of both writers not only entertain but also educate and enlighten by providing a mirror to our own lives and societies. They challenge us to think deeply about our own moral and emotional landscapes and encourage empathy, understanding, and self-reflection. The timeless wisdom embedded in the writings of Maya Angelou and William Shakespeare continues to inspire, challenge, and influence readers and writers alike, reaffirming the power of literature to transcend temporal and spatial boundaries to touch the essence of our shared human experience. Through their profound literary contributions, Angelou and Shakespeare teach us about the depths of human emotions, the complexities of life, and the enduring strength of the human spirit.

ppp

"Leonardo da Vinci's boundless curiosity bridged the worlds of art and science, showing us that disciplines are interconnected and that creativity knows no bounds. He saw the art in science and the science in art. Let his Renaissance spirit inspire us to discover and innovate without limits."

❧❧❧

NINE

Advocates of Equality: Malala Yousafzai & Susan B. Anthony

Malala Yousafzai and Susan B. Anthony, although from vastly different times and contexts, have both stood as towering figures in the struggle for equality, particularly concerning women's rights and education. Their advocacy not only challenged the status quo but also laid foundational stones for continued efforts toward gender equality and universal education.

Susan B. Anthony, born in 1820, emerged as a key figure in the American women's suffrage movement, dedicating much of her life to the cause of equal rights for women. Her activism began in a period when women were largely excluded from the political realm, but she envisioned a different, more inclusive future. Alongside her colleague Elizabeth Cady Stanton, Anthony founded the National Woman Suffrage Association, which played a pivotal role in fighting for women's right to vote. Her tireless efforts culminated in significant milestones, albeit posthumously, with the passing of the

19th Amendment to the U.S. Constitution in 1920, which granted American women the right to vote. Anthony's belief in equality was profound and unwavering, famously asserting, "Men, their rights, and nothing more; women, their rights, and nothing less."

In contrast to Anthony's 19th-century context, Malala Yousafzai's activism began in the early 21st century in Swat Valley, Pakistan, under much different circumstances. Born in 1997, Malala was thrust into activism partly by her father's influence and partly by the extreme conditions under Taliban control, which aggressively suppressed women's rights, particularly the right to education. From a young age, Malala advocated for girls' education, writing a blog under a pseudonym for the BBC detailing life under the Taliban. Her advocacy gained international attention in 2012 when she was shot by a Taliban gunman as a result of her activism. Surviving this attack only strengthened her resolve, and she continued to speak out for the right to education across the globe, becoming the youngest-ever Nobel Prize laureate in 2014. Her speech at the United Nations, where she powerfully stated, "One child, one teacher, one book, and one pen can change the world," echoed around the globe, amplifying her advocacy and inspiring a new generation to take action.

Both Anthony and Yousafzai faced immense opposition in their activism. Anthony dealt with societal norms deeply entrenched in gender discrimination, often facing arrest and public ridicule. Yousafzai faced threats to her life and displacement due to her outspoken nature in a region where female education was forbidden by militant decrees. Despite these challenges, their campaigns share a common thread of resilience and a belief in the transformative power of education and equality.

Their work has inspired legislative and cultural shifts toward greater gender equality. Anthony's advocacy laid the groundwork for women's suffrage in the United States, fundamentally altering the political landscape. Similarly, Yousafzai's efforts have not only raised global awareness about the education crisis for girls but also resulted in concrete steps like the Malala Fund, which invests in education programs in regions where girls are most likely to miss out on secondary education.

The legacies of these two advocates underline the importance of education and political rights as pathways to broader social and economic equity. They have shown that the fight for equality requires relentless perseverance, advocacy, and an unwavering commitment to justice. Both figures utilized their voices to catalyze change, demonstrating that advocacy can indeed alter the course of history.

Their stories continue to inspire movements around the world, highlighting that the struggle for equality is ongoing and reminding us of the power of determined individuals to influence global change. Their lives teach us valuable lessons about the intersection of education, gender rights, and empowerment, emphasizing that progress often requires challenging existing barriers and prejudices. The advocacy of Malala Yousafzai and Susan B. Anthony is a testament to the enduring struggle for gender equality and the critical role of education in achieving it, offering a blueprint for future generations to continue their efforts toward a more equitable world.

ppp

"Thich Nhat Hanh taught us the art of mindful living—to breathe, to walk, to eat, and to live each moment fully. His teachings remind us that peace begins within ourselves. May his gentle wisdom guide us to live deeply in the present moment, in peace and compassion."

ᗡᗡᗡ

TEN

EXPLORERS OF THE UNKNOWN: NEIL ARMSTRONG & AMELIA EARHART

Neil Armstrong and Amelia Earhart, each a pioneer in their own right, dramatically expanded the horizons of what humanity believed was possible. Their daring explorations into the unknown not only redefined geographical and astronomical boundaries but also symbolized the boundless potential of the human spirit to transcend limitations.

Amelia Earhart, born in 1897, was a trailblazer in the early days of aviation, a field then predominantly occupied by men. She became the first woman to fly solo across the Atlantic Ocean in 1932, an achievement that earned her not only the Distinguished Flying Cross but also a permanent place in the annals of history. Her adventurous spirit and relentless pursuit of her aviation goals challenged the societal norms of her time, inspiring countless women to consider new possibilities in their personal and professional lives. Earhart once eloquently stated, "The most effective way to do it, is to do it." This simple yet powerful affirmation reflects her approach to life and challenges — head-on and without hesitation.

Neil Armstrong, born in 1930, similarly pushed the limits of exploration but reached even further—beyond the confines of our planet. As the commander of NASA's Apollo 11 mission, he became the first human to step onto the moon in 1969, marking a monumental achievement in the history of human exploration. His famous words upon setting foot on the lunar surface, "That's one small step for man, one giant leap for mankind," perfectly capture the essence of the moment: a singular, courageous act that opened up new realms of possibility for all of humanity.

Both Armstrong and Earhart's exploits were driven by a combination of personal courage, technical skill, and the insatiable human desire to explore and push beyond known limits. Earhart's flying career during the early 20th century involved significant risks. Aviation was still in its infancy, with rudimentary navigation technologies and limited understanding of atmospheric science. Yet, she embraced these challenges, recognizing that each flight could bring valuable data that would contribute to the advancement of aviation science. Her disappearance in 1937 while attempting to circumnavigate the globe only adds to her legacy, underscoring the risks she was willing to take to pave the way for future explorers.

Armstrong's journey to the moon also involved unparalleled risks. Space travel, much like early aviation, was a new frontier fraught with unknown dangers. The Apollo missions required not only physical courage but immense mental fortitude and trust in the technology developed by thousands of scientists and engineers back on Earth. Armstrong's successful moon landing was a testament to what can be achieved when human ingenuity, bravery, and teamwork converge.

The legacies of Armstrong and Earhart extend beyond their immediate achievements. They have inspired generations to dream big and act boldly. Their lives remind us that exploring the unknown requires not only new technologies but also a willingness to confront fear and uncertainty. Each in their own way demonstrated that boundaries exist to be pushed and that the spirit of exploration can lead to profound discoveries and insights—about the world and about ourselves.

Moreover, their adventures have encouraged a cultural shift in how we perceive our limits and capabilities. Earhart's defiance of gender norms and Armstrong's venture into space have both played roles in expanding the scope of what is considered achievable, each contributing to a broader understanding of human potential. They have shown us that the final frontier is not necessarily a place but a mindset, a persistent belief in the possibility of overcoming obstacles that appear insurmountable.

The stories of Neil Armstrong and Amelia Earhart are not merely tales of high adventure but parables of human aspiration. They underscore the importance of setting high goals and the value of persistence and courage in achieving them. As we continue to explore new frontiers, from the depths of the ocean to the expanses of space, the legacies of these two pioneers serve as enduring inspirations, urging us to keep reaching beyond our limits to discover what lies on the far side of the possible.

ᗐᗐᗐ

"The Dalai Lama's message of compassion and forgiveness underscores the profound impact of kindness. His life teaches us that happiness is not a matter of circumstance, but of perspective. Let us embrace his call to treat all beings with the compassion we seek for ourselves."

ᐅᐅᐅ

ELEVEN

PHILOSOPHERS OF MODERNITY: SIMONE DE BEAUVOIR & FRIEDRICH NIETZSCHE

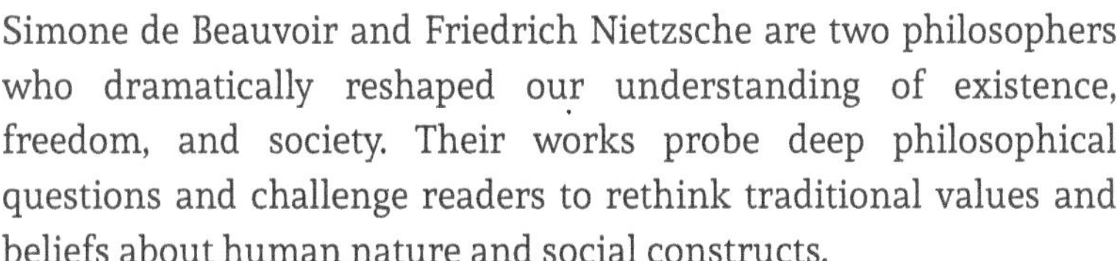

Simone de Beauvoir and Friedrich Nietzsche are two philosophers who dramatically reshaped our understanding of existence, freedom, and society. Their works probe deep philosophical questions and challenge readers to rethink traditional values and beliefs about human nature and social constructs.

Friedrich Nietzsche, a German philosopher active in the late 19th century, is perhaps best known for his provocative assertion that "God is dead," a metaphorical declaration reflecting the erosion of traditional religious and metaphysical certainties in the modern age. This statement, far from being merely an atheistic proclamation, pointed towards the larger crisis of meaning that Nietzsche saw as characteristic of modern society. He feared that the decline of religious and metaphysical frameworks would lead to nihilism, an abyss where life lacks purpose and value.

Nietzsche's philosophy is a robust call for the reevaluation of all values. His critique of morality, particularly Christian morality, is aimed at what he considered its life-denying aspects. He championed the idea of the "Übermensch" or "Overman," a figure who creates new values in the wake of the old, transcending the moral constraints and mediocrity of conventional life. Nietzsche saw the Übermensch as someone who, through sheer will and creativity, forges a life that is a work of art. His assertion that "What does not kill me, makes me stronger," encapsulates his philosophy of embracing challenges and adversities as opportunities for growth and transformation.

Simone de Beauvoir, a 20th-century French existentialist philosopher, is most celebrated for her pioneering work "The Second Sex," in which she famously declared, "One is not born, but rather becomes, a woman." This assertion underlines her thesis that female identity is largely constructed through the societal roles assigned to women, rather than inherent or biological predestinations. De Beauvoir's analysis provides a critical foundation for contemporary feminist thought and has profoundly influenced the discourse on gender, identity, and equality.

De Beauvoir's existentialist approach emphasizes the concept of freedom and the responsibility that comes with it. She argues that humans are condemned to be free—that is, thrust into existence without choice, yet free to make of it what they will. Her philosophy insists on the fundamental ambiguity of life, urging an ethics of ambiguity which recognizes the complexities of human actions and the contexts that shape them. Her discussions extend to the ethics of action, suggesting that one's freedom should be used to foster the freedom of others, thereby constructing a more just society.

Both Nietzsche and Beauvoir challenge their readers to question the "given" of their existences. Nietzsche's exploration of the depths of individual power and potential calls for a radical self-overcoming, a perpetual process of becoming that rejects passive acceptance of prescribed truths. His style of philosophy is not just a critique but an invitation to a more profound engagement with life's existential challenges.

Similarly, de Beauvoir's work invites a reevaluation of our assumptions about identity and freedom. Her analysis of women's oppression is not just an articulation of injustices but a clarion call to action. It encourages individuals, especially women, to recognize their complicity in their own oppression through accepting societal roles without question and to rise above this by asserting their freedom and agency.

The intellectual legacies of Nietzsche and de Beauvoir are both disruptive and transformative. They not only challenge individuals to think deeply about personal and societal existence but also offer visions of what it might mean to live authentically. Nietzsche's call for the revaluation of values and de Beauvoir's explication of the complexities of freedom and identity continue to resonate, urging ongoing reflection and deliberate action in the quest to understand and shape human existence in the modern world. Their philosophies empower us to critically examine our lives and the structures of our societies, inspiring profound and often uncomfortable questions about who we are and how we ought to live. Through their writings, both philosophers teach us that understanding and transforming society begins with a deep, often critical, engagement with ourselves and the world around us.

ϷϷϷ

"Muhammad Ali was more than a champion in the ring; he was a champion of civil rights and the power of conviction. His words, 'Float like a butterfly, sting like a bee,' remind us that grace and power can coexist. May his legacy encourage us to fight for what is right with both humility and strength."

ᗰᗰᗰ

TWELVE

CUSTODIANS OF PEACE: DESMOND TUTU & MOTHER TERESA

Desmond Tutu and Mother Teresa stand as towering figures of peace and humanitarianism in the 20th century, each dedicating their lives to service, compassion, and the promotion of human dignity. Their messages and actions have left indelible marks on the world, advocating for love, charity, and reconciliation as foundational principles for a better society.

Desmond Tutu, a South African Anglican bishop and a fervent anti-apartheid activist, became an international symbol of non-violent resistance and a voice for oppressed peoples. Tutu's philosophy of forgiveness and reconciliation was crucial in the transition of South Africa from a system of racial segregation to a democracy. As the chairman of the Truth and Reconciliation Commission (TRC), Tutu advocated for a restorative justice approach, which sought to heal a broken nation through truth-telling and forgiveness rather than retribution. His belief in the "Rainbow Nation" concept—a term he coined to describe post-apartheid South Africa—envisioned a multicultural country where all races were accepted and valued. One of his most profound statements, "If you want peace, you don't talk to your friends. You talk to your enemies," encapsulates his approach to achieving lasting peace through dialogue and understanding, regardless of past conflicts.

Mother Teresa, an Albanian-Indian Roman Catholic nun and missionary, became globally renowned for her charitable work with the poorest of the poor in Kolkata, India. In 1950, she founded the Missionaries of Charity, a congregation dedicated to caring for those who had nobody to look after them. Mother Teresa's life was a testament to her profound faith and commitment to her calling, which was grounded in a deep sense of love and service to others. She famously said, "Not all of us can do great things. But we can do small things with great love." This simple yet powerful message highlights her belief that universal love and charity begin with small, everyday actions accessible to every individual, irrespective of wealth or status.

Both Tutu and Mother Teresa shared a common belief in the sanctity and equality of all human life. Their life's work reflects their commitment to these principles, demonstrating that genuine peace and harmony are achieved through acts of love and compassion, not through force or coercion. They saw no division too deep or wound too severe to be healed through the power of empathetic service and honest reconciliation. Their legacies are characterized not only by their accomplishments but also by their character—humility, joy, and an unshakeable faith in the goodness of humanity.

Their teachings and lives also provide profound lessons on the nature of true service. Desmond Tutu's advocacy went beyond merely ending apartheid; he sought to foster a culture of peace and tolerance. His message encouraged others to recognize their shared humanity and to act with moral integrity and courage, particularly when addressing systemic injustice. Tutu's work with the TRC exemplifies his belief in humanity's capacity for forgiveness and redemption, emphasizing that a society's enduring peace depends on its ability to acknowledge and learn from its past.

Similarly, Mother Teresa's work with the sick and the dying highlighted the power of compassionate action to affirm the inherent worth of every individual. Her dedication to the most destitute and forgotten segments of society challenged global perceptions about poverty and the responsibilities of those more fortunate. Her actions demonstrated her conviction that charity and active compassion are among the most potent forces for social change.

The messages of Desmond Tutu and Mother Teresa resonate in today's global society, where division and indifference often overshadow calls to unity and kindness. Their lives remind us of the profound impact of dedicated service rooted in love and respect for all humanity. They challenge individuals and communities to look beyond themselves and to act towards others with generosity and understanding. In a world often marred by conflict and strife, the legacies of these two custodians of peace serve as beacons of hope, teaching us that peace starts with empathy and is sustained through committed, loving service.

ppp

"Serena Williams has redefined what it means to be a powerful woman in sports and in life. Her determination and resilience have broken barriers and set new standards. Let her tenacity inspire us to pursue our goals with unwavering spirit."

ᐁᐁᐁ

THIRTEEN

SAGES OF BUSINESS: HENRY FORD & SHERYL SANDBERG

Henry Ford and Sheryl Sandberg, though from different eras and sectors within the business world, each embody the essence of innovative and resilient leadership. Their contributions to business are not merely about financial success but include significant advancements in corporate culture, management philosophies, and leadership principles. Their careers offer timeless insights into navigating business challenges and driving change within their industries.

Henry Ford, the founder of Ford Motor Company, is often credited with revolutionizing the automotive industry by introducing assembly line manufacturing. This innovation significantly lowered the costs of production, making cars affordable for the average American and thereby democratizing automobile ownership. Ford's vision went beyond the technical aspects of his business; he also introduced the $5 a day wage for his workers—an unprecedented move at the time that doubled the standard wage. This not only reduced employee turnover but also increased productivity and gave workers the purchasing power to buy the cars they produced, thus expanding the market for his products. Ford's approach to business was marked by a focus on efficiency, innovation, and worker satisfaction. He famously stated, "Coming together is a beginning; keeping together is progress; working together is success," reflecting his belief in the importance of collaboration and mutual benefit.

On the other hand, Sheryl Sandberg, known for her role as COO of Facebook (now Meta Platforms) and her book "Lean In: Women, Work, and the Will to Lead," brought to light the challenges women face in the workplace and offered new frameworks for understanding and navigating leadership roles. Sandberg's advocacy for women in leadership has sparked broad discussions about gender equality in corporate America and beyond. Her concept of "leaning in" encourages women to embrace opportunities and challenges with confidence and assertiveness. Sandberg's leadership at Facebook was also significant for her focus on scalable business strategies and her ability to steer the company through periods of rapid growth and intense scrutiny. Her resilience was profoundly tested in personal life after the sudden death of her husband, following which she wrote "Option B," a book that explores facing adversity and building resilience.

Both Ford and Sandberg experienced setbacks and criticism in their careers, yet their responses to these challenges have been instructive. Ford faced several failed business attempts before establishing the successful Ford Motor Company. His persistence and willingness to innovate within the manufacturing process played a crucial role in his eventual success. Ford's ability to learn from past failures and continuously refine his business model and operations underscored his strategic foresight and resilience.

Similarly, Sandberg's tenure at Facebook involved navigating the company through various controversies, including issues related to privacy and misinformation. Her strategic approach often involved advocating for transparency and initiating dialogues to address public concerns proactively. Her leadership style, which emphasizes growth through learning, reflects her belief in the potential for personal and professional development even through difficulties.

Both leaders also significantly impacted corporate culture. Ford's practices around employee wages and treatment led to broader changes in how workers were valued in the industrial sector. His innovations in employee welfare set new benchmarks for what companies could do to motivate and care for their employees. In a similar vein, Sandberg's advocacy for workplace equality and her focus on mentorship and support networks have influenced how corporations structure leadership development programs and support diversity and inclusion.

The business philosophies of Henry Ford and Sheryl Sandberg provide rich lessons in leadership and management. Ford's emphasis on innovation, efficiency, and employee welfare transformed industrial manufacturing and had lasting implications on the global economy. Sandberg's focus on inclusive leadership and resilience has not only guided her company through modern challenges but also inspired a generation of women to aspire to and succeed in leadership roles.

Through their unique contributions to business and leadership, Henry Ford and Sheryl Sandberg exemplify how visionary leadership can profoundly impact an industry and society. Their careers teach us about the importance of innovation, the value of resilient and inclusive leadership, and the potential of business leaders to effect substantive, positive change in their organizations and the world at large.

ppp

"Sun Tzu's 'The Art of War' teaches that true wisdom lies in the strategy of thoughtful planning rather than in mere conquest. His insights remind us that knowledge and preparation are the keys to success. Let us apply his strategic thinking to navigate the battles we face in life."

ᛈᛈᛈ

FOURTEEN

ICONS OF COURAGE: HARRIET TUBMAN & WINSTON CHURCHILL

Harriet Tubman and Winston Churchill, figures emblematic of courage and resilience, navigated through some of the most turbulent periods in history, leaving indelible marks on their respective societies. Their lives not only exemplify personal bravery but also the capacity to inspire and lead others in the face of grave dangers.

Harriet Tubman, born into slavery in Maryland, USA, became a legendary figure in the American abolitionist movement. After escaping slavery herself, she risked her life repeatedly by returning to the South to lead dozens of enslaved people to freedom via the Underground Railroad. Tubman's courage was rooted in her deep conviction in the fight against the institution of slavery and her commitment to human dignity. Her fearless actions were driven by a profound sense of duty and justice, encapsulated in her famous declaration, "I had reasoned this out in my mind; there was one of two things I had a right to, liberty, or death; if I could not have one, I would have the other."

Winston Churchill, the British Prime Minister during the Second World War, became a symbol of resilience and defiant leadership during one of the darkest times in modern history. His leadership during the war was characterized by his remarkable ability to communicate and inspire hope in a beleaguered nation facing the onslaught of the Axis powers. His speeches are among the most powerful oratories in the English language, serving to bolster the British spirit under dire circumstances. Perhaps his most famous line, delivered during the Battle of Britain, encapsulates his indomitable spirit: "We shall fight on the beaches, we shall fight on the landing grounds, we shall fight in the fields and in the streets, we shall fight in the hills; we shall never surrender."

Both Tubman and Churchill faced seemingly insurmountable odds with a level of bravery that has become the stuff of legend. Tubman operated within the domestic borders of a country that legally sanctioned slavery, using secretive networks and taking incredible personal risks. Her operations required meticulous planning, unwavering determination, and a fearless confrontation of constant danger. Tubman's life was guided by a spiritual sense of mission, which she described as directives from God, providing her with the fortitude to lead others to freedom without ever losing a single passenger.

Churchill, on the other hand, faced the might of Nazi Germany at a time when Britain stood almost alone against it. His courage was displayed through his public presence and speeches, which were crucial in keeping public morale high. Churchill's ability to convey a message of unyielding resistance and eventual victory was vital not only to Britain's war effort but to that of the entire Allied forces. His speeches during the war did not merely describe a hope for victory; they willed it into existence by fostering a collective resolve to fight on, despite the hardships.

The legacies of Tubman and Churchill in inspiring bravery are rooted in their profound understanding of the human condition and the need for hope and courage in times of crisis. Tubman's personal sacrifice and direct action in liberating others from the shackles of slavery highlight a deeply personal type of courage. In contrast, Churchill's leadership during WWII demonstrates how courage can be mediated through powerful rhetoric and steadfast public leadership.

Their stories teach us that courage can manifest in various forms, whether on the secretive routes of the Underground Railroad or in the bomb-riddled streets of wartime Britain. Both figures utilized their unique positions to effect change, demonstrating that the heart of courage lies in the readiness to act in the face of fear, not in the absence of it.

Through their extraordinary lives, Harriet Tubman and Winston Churchill not only changed the course of history but also left a lasting legacy on how leadership and personal bravery can inspire others to rise above adversity. Their examples continue to teach future generations about the essence of bravery and the impact of courageous leadership during times of great peril.

ppp

"Warren Buffett's investment philosophy shows us that patience, discipline, and value are timeless virtues in finance and in life. He teaches us that building lasting wealth is about consistency and quality. May his pragmatic wisdom guide us to make thoughtful and informed decisions."

ᗷᗷᗷ

FIFTEEN

VOICES OF CREATIVITY: PABLO PICASSO & VIRGINIA WOOLF

Pablo Picasso and Virginia Woolf, each a pioneer in their respective fields of visual art and literature, significantly altered the landscape of 20th-century creative expression. Their work challenged traditional forms and introduced new ways of thinking about and depicting the human experience, fundamentally reshaping our understanding of art and narrative.

Pablo Picasso, a Spanish painter and sculptor, is celebrated as one of the most influential artists of the 20th century. He is best known for co-founding the Cubist movement, an artistic expression that abandoned the traditional perspectives of proportion and design, and instead emphasized abstract forms and multiple viewpoints. Picasso's approach broke away from the conventional portrayal of reality, allowing him to explore complex themes such as the fragmentation of the human form and the intersection of different realities. His famous work "Les Demoiselles d'Avignon" (1907), with its radical distortion of form and space, marked a dramatic break from traditional composition, signaling the birth of a new avant-garde aesthetic that would eventually ripple across the artistic world.

Picasso's innovation was not confined to Cubism alone; his artistic journey included periods of exploration in Surrealism, Classicism, and Expressionism, demonstrating his relentless pursuit of artistic evolution. His prolific output spans over 20,000 paintings, prints, drawings, sculptures, ceramics, theater sets, and costumes, showcasing his versatility and creative genius. His motto, "Every act of creation is first an act of destruction," captures his approach to artistic innovation—continuously deconstructing and reinventing new styles and methodologies.

Similarly, Virginia Woolf, an English writer and one of the foremost modernists of the 20th century, is known for her innovative approach to narrative structure and character development. Woolf's writing is characterized by its exploratory stream-of-consciousness technique, which seeks to depict the inner lives of her characters through their thoughts and feelings as they occur. This style marked a departure from the linear, plot-driven conventions of Victorian and Edwardian literature, offering instead a deep dive into the psychological underpinnings of personality and experience.

Woolf's novels, such as "Mrs. Dalloway" (1925) and "To the Lighthouse" (1927), illustrate her skill in using this technique to weave complex, multi-layered narratives that explore the intricacies of time, memory, and human emotion. In "Mrs. Dalloway," Woolf deftly constructs a narrative that spans across a single day in the life of Clarissa Dalloway, yet traverses back and forth in time, capturing decades of memories and experiences, thereby challenging conventional narrative timelines and perspectives. Woolf famously argued that "a woman must have money and a room of her own if she is to write fiction," highlighting her belief in the socio-economic independence needed for creative freedom.

Both Picasso and Woolf were profoundly influenced by the turbulent events of their times, including the two World Wars, which shaped their artistic outlooks and the themes they explored. Picasso's "Guernica" (1937), a dramatic and unsettling depiction of the horrors of the Spanish Civil War, uses Cubist techniques to evoke emotion and provoke thought about the tragedies of war. Similarly, Woolf's "Between the Acts" (1941) reflects the impending threat of World War II and examines the fragmentation and impending chaos looming over British society.

Picasso and Woolf's contributions go beyond their specific artistic and literary innovations. They challenged the audience to see the world differently, to question their perceptions, and to engage with complex realities that do not easily conform to traditional narratives or visual representations. Their works encourage a dialogue between the creator and the viewer or reader, a dialogue that invites a deeper engagement with the artwork and the written word.

In their relentless pursuit of new artistic expressions, Pablo Picasso and Virginia Woolf not only transformed their respective fields but also offered new ways of seeing and understanding the world. Their legacy is characterized by a continuous challenge to conventional thinking, urging generations of artists and writers to experiment and innovate in their quest to capture the essence of human experience. Through their groundbreaking works, they have permanently altered the course of art and literature, leaving an enduring impact on both creators and consumers of culture.

ɒɒɒ

"Maya Angelou's words bring a light of hope and an enduring strength that encourages us to rise above our circumstances. Her poetic voice, a blend of vigor and vulnerability, teaches us that we are all capable of greatness. Let her life remind us that we can face the world with boldness and beauty."

ᐅᐅᐅ

SIXTEEN

REVOLUTIONARIES OF THOUGHT: KARL MARX & AYN RAND

Karl Marx and Ayn Rand represent two diametrically opposed philosophies that have profoundly influenced political thought, economic theory, and individual action. Marx, a philosopher, economist, and revolutionary, is best known for his critiques of capitalism and his vision of a future communist society. Rand, a novelist and philosopher, championed individualism and capitalism, vehemently opposing any form of collectivism. Their ideas have inspired, shaped, and polarized political and economic debates around the world.

Karl Marx, co-author of "The Communist Manifesto" and author of "Das Kapital," developed a theory of history and economics that centered on the struggle between social classes. Marx argued that history was primarily a series of class struggles between the bourgeoisie (the capitalist class who owns the means of production) and the proletariat (the working class who sell their labor).

He believed that the inherent exploitation within capitalism would inevitably lead to its downfall and the rise of socialism, followed by communism—a classless, stateless society where the means of production are owned communally. Marx famously asserted, "The history of all hitherto existing society is the history of class struggles," and he called for workers of the world to unite, contending they had "nothing to lose but their chains."

Marx's critique of capitalism focuses on its inefficiencies, inherent inequalities, and its tendency to alienate individuals from the fruits of their labor, leading to a dehumanized and detached society. His work has provided the intellectual foundation for various socialist movements around the globe, influencing numerous political entities and leaders who have sought to implement his theories, often with modifications and adaptations.

In stark contrast, Ayn Rand, through her novels such as "Atlas Shrugged" and "The Fountainhead," as well as through her philosophical system of Objectivism, promoted individualism and a free-market capitalist society. Rand posited that the moral purpose of one's life is the pursuit of one's own happiness (rational self-interest), and that the only social system consistent with this morality is one that fully respects individual rights embodied in laissez-faire capitalism.

She argued vehemently against collectivism, socialism, and altruism, suggesting that they lead to the suppression of individual potential and the degradation of freedom in society. Rand's philosophy is encapsulated in her statement, "The question isn't who is going to let me; it's who is going to stop me."

Rand envisioned a society where individuals are free to pursue their own interests, free from government intervention and societal obligations that hinder personal achievement. Her protagonists, such as Howard Roark and John Galt, are paragons of entrepreneurial spirit and individualism, battling against the forces of social conformity and state control. Rand's ideas have been especially influential among libertarians and conservative thinkers in the United States, advocating for a minimal state and maximum personal freedom.

The ideologies of Marx and Rand not only propose different visions of an ideal society but also offer contrasting views on human nature, motivation, and ethics. Marx sees human fulfillment as achievable through collective action and shared ownership, arguing that a society's wealth should be distributed according to one's needs, not according to one's ability.

In contrast, Rand celebrates the creative power and potential of the individual, asserting that personal success and innovation are driven by a free, unregulated market and that wealth is a just reward for individual effort and talent.

The impacts of their thoughts are evident in various aspects of modern society—from political systems and global conflicts to personal lifestyles and ethical considerations. Marxist theory has played a crucial role in shaping the policies of countries that adopted communist ideologies, with varying outcomes and often intense debates about their successes and failures.

Rand's Objectivism has found a significant following among those who advocate for capitalism and individual rights, influencing business leaders, politicians, and academics.

The legacies of Marx and Rand, with their deep-seated beliefs and radical proposals, continue to provoke discussion and controversy. They challenge individuals to reconsider their views on justice, liberty, and the role of government in personal and economic life.

Whether one agrees with Marx's call for a classless society or Rand's advocacy for unfettered capitalism, their works compel a critical examination of our current societal structures and personal beliefs, making them enduringly relevant in the study of political and economic philosophy.

ᚦᚦᚦ

"William Shakespeare's masterful plays and sonnets capture the full spectrum of human emotion, from tragedy to joy. His profound insights into the human condition remind us that we are not so different in our experiences of love, loss, and redemption. May his timeless works inspire us to embrace our own stories with courage and honesty."

ᏢᏢᏢ

SEVENTEEN

LEGENDS OF MUSIC: BOB MARLEY & LUDWIG VAN BEETHOVEN

Bob Marley and Ludwig van Beethoven, though centuries apart and hailing from vastly different cultural backgrounds, each left an indelible mark on the world of music, crafting legacies that continue to uplift, inspire, and communicate profound truths. Their compositions and performances transcended mere entertainment, touching on universal themes of struggle, joy, and human spirit, resonating across generations and borders.

Ludwig van Beethoven, a pivotal figure in the transition between the Classical and Romantic eras in Western classical music, is celebrated not only for his compositions but also for his ability to convey deep emotion and the human experience through symphonies, sonatas, and quartets. Despite suffering from gradual hearing loss, which eventually led to total deafness, Beethoven continued to compose some of his most important works, a testament to his resilience and dedication to music. His Ninth

Symphony, which includes the famous "Ode to Joy," a hymn celebrating universal brotherhood, exemplifies his belief in music as a medium to express ideals and emotions more profound than words could convey. Beethoven once remarked, "Music is a higher revelation than all wisdom and philosophy," reflecting his view of music as a conduit for expressing the inexpressible.

Bob Marley, a reggae icon whose music was infused with spiritual and political significance, emerged as a voice for the oppressed, using his platform to champion social justice, peace, and reconciliation. Marley's lyrics, often intertwined with Rastafarian beliefs, resonate with calls for freedom and resistance against oppression, as exemplified in songs like "Redemption Song," which includes the powerful lyrics, "Emancipate yourselves from mental slavery, none but ourselves can free our minds." Marley's ability to craft songs that spoke to the struggles and hopes of the disenfranchised, while still infusing them with a sense of love and unity, made his music a rallying cry for diverse audiences around the world.

Both Beethoven and Marley explored and expanded the boundaries of their respective musical genres. Beethoven's compositions, characterized by their structural innovations and emotional depth, pushed the limits of musical expression within the classical framework. His work played a critical role in shaping the future direction of Western classical music, influencing countless composers and musicians who followed. His personal motto, "To play without passion is inexcusable," not only highlights his approach to performance and composition but also his belief in the power of music to move and stir the soul.

Similarly, Marley's innovative approach to reggae incorporated elements from rhythm and blues, rocksteady, and ska, contributing to the genre's global appeal. His performances were charismatic, infused with a sense of purpose and urgency that made his music compelling to a global audience. Marley viewed music as both a tool for social change and a spiritual force, famously stating, "One good thing about music, when it hits you, you feel no pain," underscoring his belief in music as a healing force.

The musical legacies of Beethoven and Marley continue to uplift spirits and inspire listeners. Beethoven's compositions are celebrated for their technical mastery and emotional power, often performed in concert halls as exemplary works of classical music's capacity to convey a wide range of human emotions. Marley's songs continue to be anthems of resistance and calls for peace, their relevance undiminished by the passing of time.

Both artists demonstrated that music, more than being merely sound, is a powerful form of communication that can express the ineffable, connect disparate cultures, and articulate societal conditions and aspirations. They showed that music could be a force for change, a source of consolation and joy, and a universal language that speaks to the common desires and experiences of humanity.

In sum, the legacies of Bob Marley and Ludwig van Beethoven are not only enshrined in their musical innovations and acclaimed compositions but also in their profound impact on society and the arts. Through their creative genius, they have shown how music can uplift, heal, and mobilize, carrying messages of depth and truth across generations. Their contributions continue to inspire artists and audiences alike, proving that music has the enduring power to transform hearts and minds.

♪♪♪

"The voices of history's legends echo through time, reminding us that perseverance is the companion of success. They inspire us with tales of overcoming adversity, not through the absence of failure, but through the persistence of courage. Let their stories embolden us to face our challenges with determination, knowing that each step forward is a victory in itself."

▷▷▷

EIGHTEEN

TRAILBLAZERS OF FEMINISM: GLORIA STEINEM & EMMELINE PANKHURST

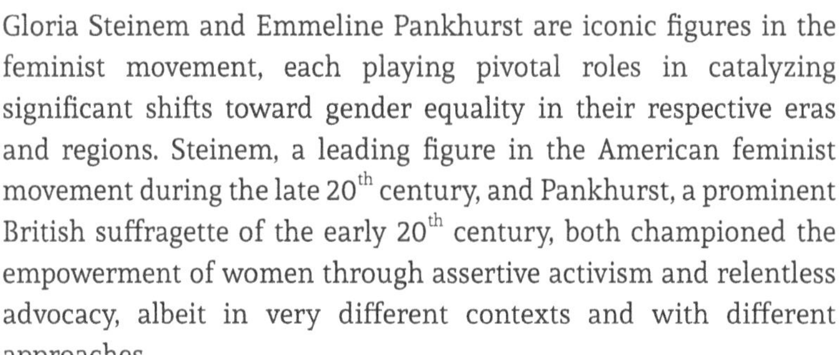

Gloria Steinem and Emmeline Pankhurst are iconic figures in the feminist movement, each playing pivotal roles in catalyzing significant shifts toward gender equality in their respective eras and regions. Steinem, a leading figure in the American feminist movement during the late 20th century, and Pankhurst, a prominent British suffragette of the early 20th century, both championed the empowerment of women through assertive activism and relentless advocacy, albeit in very different contexts and with different approaches.

Emmeline Pankhurst founded the Women's Social and Political Union (WSPU) in the UK in 1903, an organization known for its militant tactics aimed at securing women's suffrage. Pankhurst's approach to the movement was characterized by her motto, "Deeds, not words," reflecting her belief that dramatic actions were necessary to achieve political change. Under her leadership, the suffragettes used unconventional and controversial methods, including chaining themselves to railings, smashing windows, and enduring hunger strikes, to draw attention to their cause. These actions were met with severe criticism and often violent responses, yet they succeeded in keeping women's suffrage in the public and political spotlight, ultimately contributing to women gaining the right to vote in the UK.

Pankhurst's determination was rooted in her conviction that women's inferior status in society prevented them from effectively advocating for themselves and their families on issues including poverty and child welfare. Her activism was not without personal cost; she faced multiple imprisonments and endured harsh conditions that impacted her health. Pankhurst's legacy is a testament to her unyielding dedication to the cause of women's rights, embodying the struggle for political equality in a society that was initially resistant to change.

In contrast, Gloria Steinem emerged as a key figure in the American feminist movement during the 1960s and 1970s, a period marked by a surge in feminist activism focused on issues such as abortion rights, equal employment, and social justice. Steinem's approach combined journalism with activism; she co-founded "Ms. Magazine," a groundbreaking publication that provided a platform for feminist voices and issues. Steinem's activism extended beyond publication; she was instrumental in founding the National Women's Political Caucus, which is dedicated to increasing the number of women in all aspects of political life.

Steinem's message emphasized the importance of women's autonomy over their bodies and their lives, famously stating, "A woman without a man is like a fish without a bicycle," to underscore the idea that women do not require men to define their existence or capabilities. Her advocacy extended to a broad critique of societal norms that dictated gender roles, arguing for a redefinition of what it meant to be a woman in modern society. Steinem worked to build a more inclusive feminist movement, recognizing the diverse and intersectional identities of women, including race, class, and sexual orientation, which influenced the course of feminist theory and activism.

Both Pankhurst and Steinem faced significant opposition and criticism, yet their work had a profound impact on the feminist movement and on society's understanding of gender equality. Pankhurst's militant tactics helped to break the initial barriers to discussing women's suffrage in the public and political arena, setting the stage for subsequent legal and societal changes. Meanwhile, Steinem's advocacy and media work broadened the scope of feminist issues, making them part of the national conversation in the United States and influencing public policies related to women's rights.

The legacies of Emmeline Pankhurst and Gloria Steinem highlight their roles as trailblazers who reshaped societal views about women's roles and rights. Through their determined and visionary leadership, they not only advanced the rights of women in their respective countries but also inspired generations of feminists around the world to continue the fight for equality. Their lives and work demonstrate the power of committed activism to challenge and change entrenched social norms and to empower women to claim their rights and rightful place in society.

ϼϼϼ

"Legends teach us that greatness is often a quiet
journey, marked not by fanfare but by steadfast
resolve and humble dedication. Their motivations,
distilled through time, serve as a beacon, guiding us
toward our own paths of excellence. Embrace their
wisdom, and let it fuel your journey toward
achieving your own legendary status."

▷▷▷

NINETEEN

PIONEERS OF SCIENCE: ALBERT EINSTEIN & RACHEL CARSON

Albert Einstein and Rachel Carson are distinguished figures in the annals of science, each pioneering significant shifts not only in scientific thought but also in our understanding of humanity's relationship with the natural world. Their contributions went beyond mere academic inquiry; they challenged and expanded the societal implications of scientific discoveries, advocating for a deeper responsibility towards our environment and our understanding of the universe.

Albert Einstein, one of the most celebrated physicists of the 20th century, revolutionized our understanding of the nature of the universe. His theory of relativity fundamentally altered the way we perceive space and time, introducing concepts such as the curvature of space-time and the relativity of simultaneity. Einstein's equation, $E=mc^2$, which posits that energy and mass are interchangeable, reshaped the foundational principles of physics, influencing everything from nuclear power generation to our understanding of cosmic phenomena. His curiosity about the observable universe's laws led to profound insights that not only advanced scientific knowledge but also contributed to a broader philosophical understanding of how we observe and interact with our surroundings.

Einstein's impact extended beyond the theoretical; his reflections on science's role in society and the ethical implications of scientific discoveries prompted deeper consideration of technology's role in shaping human affairs. He famously warned of the dangers of nuclear weapons following their development, which had been made possible by his own equations. His quote, "The release of atomic power has changed everything except our way of thinking..." underscores his perspective on the need for a shift in societal values and responsibilities in the atomic age. Einstein believed in the importance of using scientific knowledge to foster peace and safeguard humanity, reflecting his deep moral commitment to the betterment of society.

In parallel, Rachel Carson, a marine biologist and conservationist, is credited with advancing the global environmental movement through her groundbreaking work, "Silent Spring." Published in 1962, the book detailed the adverse effects of indiscriminate pesticide use, particularly DDT, on wildlife and human health. Carson's meticulous research and engaging narrative exposed the ecological and health repercussions of chemical pollutants, challenging the practices of agricultural scientists and the chemical industry.

"Silent Spring" catalyzed a significant shift in public awareness about environmental issues and the interconnectedness of all living organisms. Carson's work laid the foundation for the modern environmental movement, leading to policy changes and the eventual ban of DDT in the United States. Her ability to communicate complex scientific ideas in clear, vivid language made the science accessible and compelling to a general audience, underscoring her skill as both a scientist and a writer. Carson once stated, "In nature, nothing exists alone," a reminder of the ecological interconnectedness and the importance of maintaining the environmental integrity for all species' survival.

Both Einstein and Carson exemplified how scientific curiosity coupled with a sense of moral duty could have far-reaching effects on society and public policy. Einstein's contributions invited us to rethink our place in the universe and the potential consequences of scientific advancements, while Carson's efforts fostered a greater appreciation for the environmental costs of human economic activities.

Their legacies are not just of scientific discovery, but of prompting a broader dialogue about the ethical use of scientific knowledge and our responsibilities towards each other and our planet. They demonstrated that the true value of scientific inquiry lies not only in its ability to expand our understanding of the world but also in its potential to improve the conditions of life on Earth. Through their work, Einstein and Carson each called for a conscientious application of scientific knowledge, advocating for a world where curiosity about nature and responsibility for its preservation go hand in hand. Their insights continue to inspire new generations of scientists and environmentalists to explore, understand, and responsibly act in our complex and ever-changing world.

ppp

"The motivational words of historical legends are not merely echoes of the past but calls to action in the present. They remind us that every moment holds the potential for us to be catalysts of change. Inspired by their enduring spirits, let us seize our days with vigor and vision, striving to craft a legacy that is both impactful and inspiring."

ppp

TWENTY

HUMANITARIANS OF HOPE: ELIE WIESEL & KOFI ANNAN

Elie Wiesel and Kofi Annan, though they hailed from different backgrounds and traversed different paths, each became a symbol of hope and humanity, advocating passionately for peace, justice, and human dignity. Their lives and careers were marked by profound commitments to addressing human suffering and promoting a deeper understanding of humanity's potential for both cruelty and compassion.

Elie Wiesel, a Holocaust survivor, author, and Nobel Peace Prize laureate, dedicated his life to ensuring that the world would never forget the atrocities committed during World War II, and to fighting against human rights abuses worldwide. Wiesel's experiences in the Nazi concentration camps, where he lost much of his family, shaped his profound sense of responsibility to speak for those who could not. His literary works, particularly the seminal "Night," serve as poignant testaments to the horrors of the Holocaust and the enduring spirit of survival. His declaration that "to remain silent and indifferent is the greatest sin of all" stands as a compelling call to action against apathy and injustice. Wiesel's advocacy went beyond remembrance; he used his experiences as foundations for broader ethical and moral arguments against all forms of tyranny and oppression, championing the cause of peace throughout his life.

Kofi Annan, a Ghanaian diplomat who served as the Secretary-General of the United Nations, was another towering figure in international politics, known for his quiet diplomacy and his firm belief in the UN as a force for good. During his tenure, Annan sought to revitalize the United Nations and to bring it closer to the global public by advocating for democratic principles and human rights. His efforts to combat HIV/AIDS, his push for the development of the Millennium Development Goals, and his involvement in peacekeeping operations underscored his commitment to improving global welfare. Annan believed deeply in the power of dialogue over conflict and often emphasized the importance of understanding and cooperation across cultures and nations. His often-quoted insight, "We may have different religions, different languages, different colored skin, but we all belong to one human race," perfectly encapsulates his vision of a united global community.

Both Wiesel and Annan experienced and understood great suffering and injustice, yet they used their positions to advocate for a world where such pain might be ameliorated. Wiesel, through his powerful writings and speeches, illuminated the darkest sides of human nature and history, urging the world to recognize its capacity for evil and to actively choose a different path. He challenged individuals and leaders alike to confront cruelty and indifference with vigilance and moral courage.

Similarly, Annan's diplomatic efforts were driven by his conviction that peace and security are achievable only through cooperation and mutual understanding. His leadership at the United Nations was marked by a pragmatic approach to conflict resolution and a persistent optimism about the role of international organizations in fostering global solidarity. Annan's legacy, particularly his concept of a "responsibility to protect," has shaped international responses to humanitarian crises, emphasizing the global community's obligation to intervene when national governments fail to protect their own citizens from atrocities.

The enduring messages of hope and humanity championed by Wiesel and Annan are particularly resonant in times of adversity. They remind us that the actions of individuals and communities matter profoundly, that memory and dialogue are vital tools in the struggle against forgetting and complacency, and that our common humanity must be the foundation of our actions and policies. Their lives exemplify the belief that hope is not naïve; it is a necessary condition for the pursuit of peace and justice.

Through their writings, speeches, and leadership, Elie Wiesel and Kofi Annan have inspired generations to work towards a world that embraces compassion, recognizes its shared humanity, and actively works to protect those values. Their legacies challenge us to continue advocating for a just and humane world, reflecting their unshakeable belief in the possibility of healing and renewal amidst the deepest despair.

ppp

"Bob Marley's music, rich with rhythms and infused with a message of unity and resistance, urges us to fight for our rights while loving one another. His lyrics, 'Emancipate yourselves from mental slavery, none but ourselves can free our minds,' challenge us to liberate ourselves through self-awareness and truth. Let his songs inspire us to live in harmony and stand firm against injustice. As we groove to the beat of his reggae tunes, let us remember the power of music as a tool for social change and personal enlightenment. Marley's legacy teaches us that peace and resilience can coexist, urging us to create a world where compassion and strength are intertwined."

♭♭♭

TWENTY-ONE
SUMMARY

This summary encapsulates the lives and contributions of 40 legendary figures across 20 thematic chapters, each delving into their profound impacts on society, culture, politics, science, and art. The figures discussed have left indelible marks on history, providing timeless lessons on leadership, creativity, perseverance, and human rights.

The Power of Possibility: Nelson Mandela & Helen Keller

Mandela and Keller demonstrated how overcoming immense personal and societal challenges can provide profound insights into hope and resilience, inspiring others to surmount their difficulties through courage and determination.

Visionaries of Change: Mahatma Gandhi & Martin Luther King Jr.

Gandhi and King led transformative social movements through non-violent resistance, emphasizing love and peaceful protest to combat systemic injustices, thereby reshaping societal norms and fostering new standards of civil rights.

Pioneers of Innovation: Steve Jobs & Marie Curie

Jobs and Curie revolutionized their respective fields, technology and science, showing that innovation coupled with perseverance leads to groundbreaking advancements that can profoundly impact society and industry.

Artists of Life: Frida Kahlo & Leonardo da Vinci

Kahlo and da Vinci explored the complexities of human existence and emotion through their art, pushing the boundaries of traditional forms to better capture the human experience in all its rawness and beauty.

Warriors of Mindfulness: Thich Nhat Hanh & Dalai Lama

These spiritual leaders taught the importance of compassion and mindfulness in achieving personal peace and greater societal harmony, advocating for a kinder, more empathetic world.

Champions of Willpower: Muhammad Ali & Serena Williams

Ali and Williams exemplified the power of self-belief and discipline in reaching the pinnacle of sports, using their platforms to inspire and advocate for social change and gender equality.

Strategists of Success: Sun Tzu & Warren Buffett

Sun Tzu and Buffett, through their strategic insights into military tactics and investment, respectively, have taught essential lessons on decision-making, risk management, and planning for long-term success.

Masters of Literature: Maya Angelou & William Shakespeare

Angelou and Shakespeare enriched literature with their deep explorations of the human condition, providing narratives that speak to fundamental truths about identity, society, and the human spirit.

Advocates of Equality: Malala Yousafzai & Susan B. Anthony

Yousafzai and Anthony fought tirelessly for women's rights and education, challenging oppressive structures and advocating for equality, significantly advancing the global discourse on gender and education.

Explorers of the Unknown: Neil Armstrong & Amelia Earhart

Armstrong and Earhart pushed the boundaries of human exploration, their courageous voyages into the unknown inspiring mankind to dream big and venture beyond comfort zones.

Philosophers of Modernity: Simone de Beauvoir & Friedrich Nietzsche

Beauvoir and Nietzsche provided deep philosophical insights that challenged societal norms and encouraged a more profound understanding of existence, morality, and the social constructs.

Custodians of Peace: Desmond Tutu & Mother Teresa

Tutu and Mother Teresa dedicated their lives to advocating for peace and helping the marginalized, embodying the virtues of love, charity, and forgiveness in their humanitarian efforts.

Sages of Business: Henry Ford & Sheryl Sandberg

Ford and Sandberg revolutionized business practices and leadership, promoting innovative industrial and managerial philosophies that have shaped contemporary business practices and leadership roles.

Icons of Courage: Harriet Tubman & Winston Churchill

Tubman and Churchill, through their resilient and bold leadership during times of great peril, demonstrated that courage and steadfastness can overcome tremendous adversities and inspire whole nations.

Voices of Creativity: Pablo Picasso & Virginia Woolf

Picasso and Woolf each challenged and transformed their artistic landscapes through innovative approaches to painting and writing, influencing countless artists and reshaping cultural perceptions.

Revolutionaries of Thought: Karl Marx & Ayn Rand

Marx and Rand offered sharply contrasting ideologies that have each, in their way, shaped economic and political thought, championing different paths towards human freedom and societal structure.

Legends of Music: Bob Marley & Ludwig van Beethoven

Marley and Beethoven, through their music, communicated powerful messages of unity, hope, and human emotion, transcending cultural and temporal boundaries to touch the hearts of millions.

Trailblazers of Feminism: Gloria Steinem & Emmeline Pankhurst

Steinem and Pankhurst were instrumental in advocating for women's rights, challenging legal and societal barriers to gender equality, and inspiring generations to continue the fight for equality.

Pioneers of Science: Albert Einstein & Rachel Carson

Einstein and Carson changed how we understand the universe and our impact on the environment, their scientific insights urging a deeper sense of responsibility towards our planet and its future.

Humanitarians of Hope: Elie Wiesel & Kofi Annan

Wiesel and Annan, through their dedication to humanitarian causes and peace, taught the world about the importance of remembering past atrocities and working diligently towards a future of peace and respect for human rights.

Each of these figures exemplifies the incredible impact that individuals can have on their worlds, challenging existing conditions and inspiring change through courage, innovation, and a deep commitment to justice and human rights. Their legacies continue to influence and inspire new generations to think critically about their roles in shaping a better future.

ppp

Other Books Of The Author

1. Empowering Minds: A Journey into Women's Self-Discovery and Power
2. The Dynamics of Motivation: Catalyzing Thought into Action
3. Meditation and Mental Well Being: The Path to Inner Peace and Clarity
4. The Psychology of Child Education: Nurturing Future Generations
5. Ethical Enlightenment: A Modern Guide to Living with Integrity
6. Voices of Empowerment: Stories of Women Rising Against Odds
7. Social Psychology in Everyday Life: Understanding Human Connections
8. The Essence of Motivational Speaking: Inspiring Change in Others
9. Balancing Acts: Women, Work, and the Will to Lead
10. Guiding with Grace: Raising Children with Compassion and Awareness
11. The Power of Positive Aging: Embracing Life After Fifty
12. Building Resilient Communities: Social Work in Action
13. The Ethical Educator: Principles for Teaching and Learning
14. From Insight to Impact: Social Psychology for a Better World
15. The Ethics of Empathy: A Guide to Ethical Living
16. The Science of Empowering the Self: Navigating Life's Challenges with Psychological Wisdom
17. The Mindful Conscious Leader: Meditation Techniques for Modern Management
18. Pioneering Spirit: Women's Pathways to Leadership and Empowerment
19. Feeling to Healing: The Role of Emotional Intelligence in Child Development
20. Transformative Talks and Words of Inspiration: Insights into Motivational Oratory

ඊඊඊ

Citation And References

This book represents the culmination of extensive research and meticulous analysis, incorporating a diverse range of sources, including numerous books, scholarly studies, and personal experiences. Additionally, I have scoured various websites to gather relevant information and data essential for the compilation of this work. I have taken every precaution to ensure the accuracy of the information presented and have diligently cited all sources to acknowledge their contributions.

Despite these efforts, the possibility of inadvertent errors remains. I deeply value the insights of my readers and appreciate any feedback that can help identify and rectify such inaccuracies. I encourage you to bring any discrepancies to my attention.

Your feedback is not only welcome but crucial, as it will aid in correcting current editions and enhancing the content of future ones. I am committed to maintaining the highest standards of accuracy and reliability in my work and thank you for your support and understanding.

Additionally, I firmly uphold the principle of freedom of speech and expression as guaranteed under Article 19(1)(a) of the Constitution of India, and I respect the diverse viewpoints and expressions of all readers.

ᕕᕕᕕ

Contact

Dr. Minakshi Bansal
Social Activist
Ahmedabad, Gujarat, Bharat
minakshiindiag20@yahoo.com

ᐳᐳᐳ

|| LOKAHA SAMASTHAHA SUKHINO BHAVANTU ||

• 133 •

www.ingramcontent.com/pod-product-compliance
Lightning Source LLC
Chambersburg PA
CBHW030859120726
48008CB00002B/51